MACHINES AT WORK >>>

Tractors

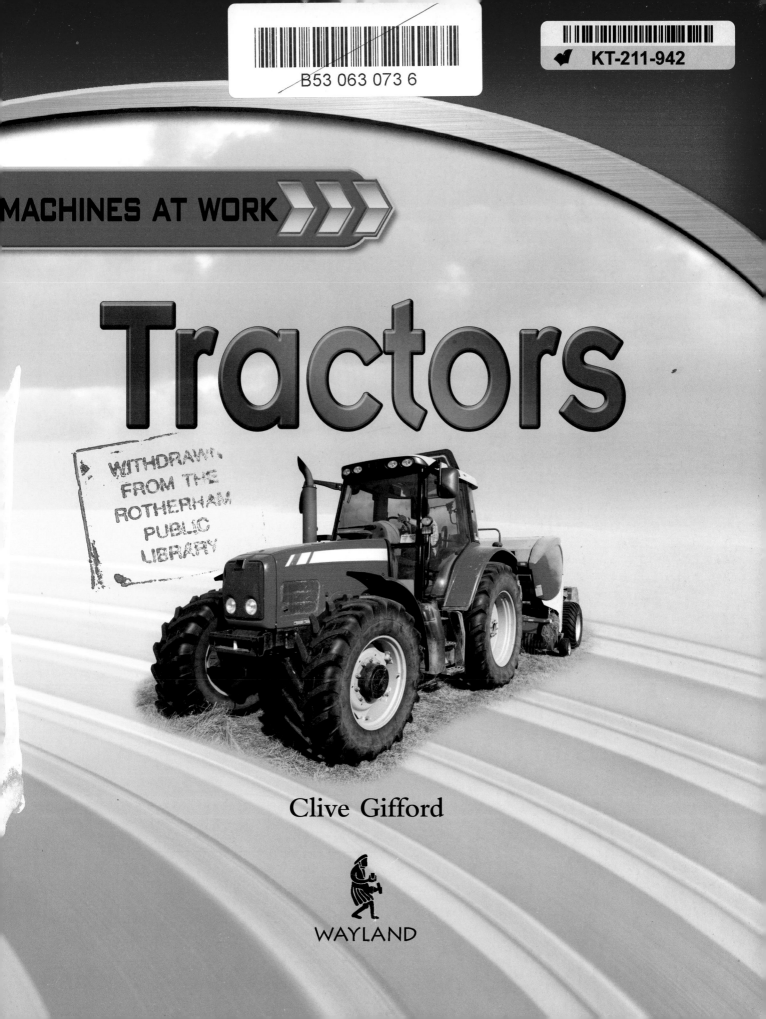

Clive Gifford

WAYLAND

Published in 2013 by Wayland
Copyright © Wayland 2013

Wayland
338 Euston Road
London NW1 3BH

Wayland Australia
Level 17/207 Kent Street
Sydney, NSW 2000

Editor: Nicola Edwards
Designer: Elaine Wilkinson
Picture Researcher: Clive Gifford

British Library Cataloguing in Publication
Data

Gifford, Clive.
   Tractors. -- (Machines at work)
   1. Farm tractors--Juvenile literature.
   I. Title II. Series
   629.2'252-dc23

ISBN: 978 0 7502 7803 4

10 9 8 7 6 5 4 3 2 1

Printed in China

Wayland is a division of Hachette Children's
Books, an Hachette UK company
www.hachette.co.uk

To find out about the author, visit his website:
www.clivegifford.co.uk

Picture acknowledgements: The author and
publisher would like to thank the following
for allowing their pictures to be reproduced
in this publication: Cover (main) Shutterstock
©: NanoStock; (inset) iStock © julia lidauer;
pp2-3 Shutterstock ©: Elena Elisseeva; p4
Shutterstock ©: Rihardzz; p5(t) Shutterstock
© Rihardzz, (b) © Wayne Hutchinson/
AgStock Images/Corbis; p6 Shutterstock
© Krivosheev Vitaly; p7 (t) Shutterstock
© Luis Louro, (b) AFP/Getty Images; p8
Shutterstock © Lucarelli Temistocle; p9(t)
© Tony Hertz/AgStock Images/Corbis,
(b) Shutterstock © Federico Rostagno; p10
Space Factory / Shutterstock.com; p11(t)
Stanislaw Tokarski / Shutterstock.com, (b)
Shutterstock © Graham Taylor; p12 iStock ©
Lya Cattel; p13(t) Shutterstock ©DeshaCAM,
(b) Shutterstock ©Leonid Ikan; p14. iStock
© Steven Robertson; p15(t) iStock ©
Cameron Pashak, (b); Shutterstock ©Mikhail
Malyshev; p16 (l) Rui Manuel Teles Gomes
/ Shutterstock.com, (r) © Paulo Fridman/
Corbis; p17 Shutterstock © Palto; p18
Shutterstock © Stephen Mcsweeny; p19(t)
Shutterstock © JP Chretien, (b) Shutterstock
© Tish1; p20 Shutterstock © lculig ; p21 (t)
ruzanna / Shutterstock.com, (b) AFP/Getty
Images; p22 Space Factory / Shutterstock.
com; p23 iStock © Cameron Pashak; p24
Shutterstock © Krivosheev Vitaly

Contents

Tractors at work

Tractors are vehicles with powerful engines and large, chunky tyres. They can travel on roads at low speeds but mostly operate in fields and on farms. All over the world, tens of thousands of tractors are busy at work.

FAST FACT

The first factory-made tractor, the Fordson, went on sale in the United States in 1917.

Engine underneath body panels

Headlights allow the tractor to work in the dark

A tractor drives through a field of hay. It tows a machine which turns the loose hay into blocks called bales.

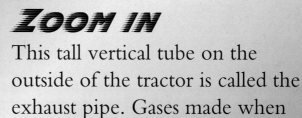

ZOOM IN

This tall vertical tube on the outside of the tractor is called the exhaust pipe. Gases made when the engine burns its fuel leave the tractor through this pipe.

The cab is where the driver sits and operates the tractor

Tractors are useful machines as they can perform many different jobs. They can pull a wide range of tools behind them. For example, on farms, tractors pull ploughs which dig up the soil ready for planting.

This tractor is pulling a potato planting machine. The machine plants seed potatoes and covers them with a layer of soil. The seed potatoes will grow into potato plants.

Large back wheels covered in rubber tyres

Getting a grip

A tractor's wheels are driven by the engine. As the wheels turn, they move the tractor forward. The force of friction helps the tyres to grip the ground.

FAST FACT

The TM1000 is one of the world's largest tractor tyres. At 2.3m high, it is taller than an adult man.

This tractor is a two-wheel-drive model. This means that only one pair of wheels, the rear ones, are driven by the engine.

axle

Large rear wheel joined to other back wheel by a bar called an axle

ZOOM IN

The pattern on a tyre is called the tread. Tractor tyres have a very chunky tread which helps them to grip the ground well.

A tractor works much of the time on rough ground or in muddy fields. Its large tyres are filled with air. Their big size means that the weight of the tractor is spread over a larger area. This helps to stop the tractor sinking into the soil or mud.

This tractor works in paddy fields where rice is grown under water. The tractor's rear wheels are made of steel frames which travel through water and grip the ground well.

Driving a tractor

A tractor cab contains several controls. A foot pedal called an accelerator or throttle makes the tractor speed up. The brake pedal slows it down. Drivers use the steering wheel to turn the tractor to the left or right or to make it go straight on.

When the driver turns the steering wheel to the right, the front wheels of the tractor turn to the right.

Many tractors can make tight turns. This is useful when a tractor has finished working on one row of crops and has to turn sharply to drive back along the next row.

This tractor is spraying rows of crops with chemicals to improve their growth. The driver has to steer carefully so that the tyres do not crush the plants.

Pulling power

A tractor is driven by a powerful engine. The engine generates enough force not only to move the tractor itself but also to tow something heavy behind it, such as a trailer on wheels with a large load. This makes a tractor a very useful vehicle to have on a farm.

FAST FACT

The Big Bud 747 is the world's largest farm tractor. It weighs over 45,000kg and its fuel tank holds 3,785 litres of fuel.

A tractor tows a trailer piled high with timber along a track in India. Other trailers may hold hay bales, fruit such as apples or fertiliser to enrich the soil.

Tractors can use their pulling power to do a variety of work. They can tow farm tools behind them, drag unwanted tree stumps out of the ground or haul other vehicles that are stuck in mud or water to safety.

ZOOM IN

A tractor's bonnet lifts up to reveal its engine. Tractor engines usually burn a type of fuel called diesel made from oil.

This crawler tractor has tracks like a tank or bulldozer instead of wheels. These grip the sand well, allowing it to tow a heavy lifeboat out of the sea.

Ploughing and planting

Most tractors have a set of links at the back to allow different tools to be attached and towed behind the vehicle. Some of these tools turn over the earth in a field and prepare it for planting seeds.

A mouldboard turns over the sliced earth

A plough has large metal blades. These cut into the ground and slice it up.

ZOOM IN

A tractor drags a tool called a harrow over a ploughed field. The harrow's rows of metal discs break down large lumps of earth into smaller clumps, ready for planting seeds.

When the field is ready, a tractor travels over it again, this time towing a seed drill. The seed drill makes grooves in the soil and then drops seeds into them. A series of spikes or bars cover the planted seeds with soil.

Hopper holds the seeds

A tractor tows a seed drill which plants seeds that will grow into crops.

Bar drags soil back over the seeds

Mowing and baling

Many tractors work in grassy fields where they mow the grass and shape it into packages that can be stored as hay. Others cut the stalks of cereal crops such as wheat and rye to form straw. Hay and straw are used as bedding and food for horses and farm animals such as cows and pigs.

This tractor tows a mower behind it. As mower's sharp blades turn they cut the grass, which will be left to dry as hay.

Once the hay or straw is dry, tractors are at work again, towing balers. These machines gather up the hay or straw and bundle it into large packages called bales.

Baler opens at the back

Completed round bale of hay drops out

Inside this baler, rollers called drums have rolled the hay into a large round shape.

ZOOM IN

Bales can be rectangle-shaped or round. Either way, they are easy for tractors to handle and store in tall stacks.

Lifters and loaders

Some tractors are used around farms, forests and other places to lift and carry all sorts of loads – from piles of soil to root vegetables such as turnips. To perform these tasks, special tools are fixed to the tractor.

Many tractors are fitted with loaders. These have a long pair of arms called a boom and a large trough at the end called a bucket. The bucket can scoop up all sorts of things from rock and stone to crops or manure.

This tractor has been fitted with a lifting tool to pick up and carry large bales of hay. The tool can be moved up and down by a lever in the driver's cab.

ZOOM IN

Bale spikes on the end of a lifter or loader plunge into a hay bale. Friction between the spikes and hay makes the spikes grip the bale well for lifting and carrying.

A Brazilian farm worker pushes coffee beans into the bucket of a tractor loader. The tractor will carry the heavy load to the farm, where the beans will be put into sacks.

Combine harvesters

When crops are fully grown, they have to be harvested. Cereal crops, such as wheat and barley, contain lots of grains which grow on long stalks. The stalks have to be cut and the useful grain has to be separated from the rest of the plant. This is all done inside a machine called a combine harvester.

Grain tank can store hundreds of kg of grain

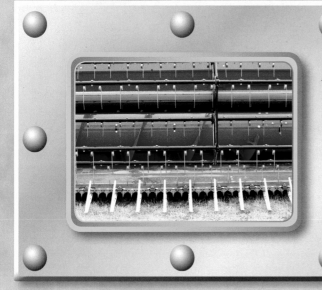

ZOOM IN

The front part of a combine harvester, the reel, spins round. It is covered in metal spikes, called tines, which push the stalks into the harvester to be cut.

Inside the combine, the grain is shaken off the stalks and is stored in the large grain tank. The stalks are pushed out of the back of the harvester as straw.

Once all the grain has been separated, it travels out of this long arm called a boom into a big container towed by a tractor driving alongside. The tractor tows away the grain for storage in a dry barn.

Driver has clear view of field from the cab

Large reel at front gathers in stalks

A combine harvester at work. It can harvest a large field of wheat in less than an hour.

Away from the fields

Tractors are such useful vehicles that they are found at work in many places other than farms. For example, smaller tractors are used in parks and on golf courses for digging, mowing and reseeding grass and for pulling out tree stumps.

This tractor is helping to clear snow away from a road. It has been fitted with a tool called a bucket excavator. This can scoop up snow and dump it away from the road.

Two tractors combine their pulling power to tow a large truck carrying hay bales out of a flooded area of land.

A tractor's pulling power can be used to tow many things besides farm tools. Tractors can pull smaller fishing boats out of the sea and up a beach. Some tractors even take part in power pulling contests. The tractor that can pull a very heavy weight the furthest is the winner.

ZOOM IN

This tractor is pulling a carnival float at a festival in the city of Limassol in Cyprus. The float contains an entire orchestra!

Quiz

So, how much do you know about tractors? Try this quick quiz to find out!

1. What is the most common fuel used to power tractor engines?
a) kerosene
b) diesel
c) paraffin

2. What farm tool is towed by a tractor to break up earth dug up by a plough?
a) harrow
b) muckspreader
c) seed drill

3. What part of a combine harvester tips grain into a trailer or hopper?
a) the reel
b) the boom
c) the cab

4. When did the first factory-made tractor go on sale?
a) 1817
b) 1857
c) 1917

5. What device sticks into a block of hay to lift it up and then carry it?
a) bale spike

b) bucker loader
c) hopper

6. What is the name of the largest farm tractor in the world?
a) the Giant 920
b) the Enormotrac 45000c
c) the Big Bud 747

7. What is the name of the container that holds all the seeds in a seed drill?
a) drum
b) hopper
c) boom

8. What name is given to the container that stores grain inside a combine harvester?
a) grain tank
b) grain boom
c) grain reel

Glossary

bales round, square or rectangular packages of hay

brakes parts of a tractor that slow the vehicle's wheels down

cab the part of a tractor where the driver sits and operates the vehicle's controls

crawler tractor a tractor equipped with tracks or treads

crops plants grown in a farm's fields

engine the part of the tractor that generates power to turn the vehicle's wheels

fertiliser a substance added to the soil to help it grow more crops

friction the force that slows movement between two objects which rub together

fuel petrol, diesel or another substance burned in an engine to create power to make the vehicle go

harvest to collect a crop from the fields of a farm

manure waste droppings from animals, often mixed with their straw bedding, which can be used in farm fields to make the soil richer

navigation system a device which helps a tractor drive accurately in the right direction

plough a farm tool towed by a tractor that breaks up the ground of a field

tonne a measure of weight equal to 1,000kg

tread the pattern of grooves on the surface of a tyre

Further Information

Books

On The Go: Tractors David and Penny Glover, Wayland, 2009
Machines On The Move: Tractors James Nixon, Franklin Watts, 2010
Machines Rule: On The Farm Steve Parker, Franklin Watts, 2011

Websites

http://www.deere.com/wps/dcom/en_US/corporate/our_
company/fans_visitors/kids/kids.page?
*The kids section of the famous American tractor maker's website has games
and videos showing tractors at work.*

http://www.williamsbigbud.com/
Learn lots more about the world's biggest farm tractor, the Big Bud 747, at this website.

http://www.youtractor.com/
A large, searchable, collection of videos of tractors and combine harvesters in action.

http://www.tractorpulling.co.uk/about.htm
Learn more about the fun sport of tractor pulling at this website.

Places To Visit

Oakham Treasures
Oakham Farm, Portbury Lane, Portbury, Bristol BS20 7Shttp://www.oakhamtreasures.co.uk/
Home to an amazing collection of 150 old tractors not just from Britain but from all over the world.

Index